Debbie Duncan's books are a word in season, speaking directly into our anxious culture. She retells Bible stories through the lens of emotion, in a lively and accessible way. The brilliant, two-tiered approach means that both little ones and older children alike will come away with a greater grasp of their emotional and mental well-being.

Katharine Hill, *UK Director of Care for the Family*

Adults and children will find this series thought-provoking and encouraging in exploring how we deal with feelings. We often hide from negative emotions, so books that help children face them, talk and pray about them, are an invaluable resource to promote emotional well-being.

Sue Monckton-Rickett, *Chair of the Association of Christian Counsellors*

Despite the increased focus on mental well-being around us, we rarely consider the emotional challenges of characters in the Bible. And yet, their feelings and responses are so helpful for us as we navigate our own obstacles and opportunities. This series gives parents and adults the tools to dig deeper with children and young people, enabling them to relate and learn from the valuable truths and experiences found in these much loved stories. These books will build emotional resilience and strong faith – and are great fun to read. What's not to love?

Cathy Madavan, *Speaker, author, and Kyria Network board member*

According to Barnardo's one in ten children have a diagnosable mental health condition and many, while they are undiagnosed, are unhappy and anxious for many reasons in today's world. Early intervention is vital before their feelings become more problematic. Debbie's God Cares series offers a gentle in-road for parents and carers to encourage them to open up about what they are feeling and what is going on in their lives. Learning early on how much God loves them and cares for them can only be a positive. Seeing their own feelings in well-known Bible characters will show them that no matter what the circumstance, God always wins!

Karen Lennie, *Cognitive Behavioural Psychotherapist PG Dip BABCP Member (Accred)*

To Sophie and Josh, my godchildren.
May you grow up knowing Jesus is always with you.

Text copyright © 2020 Debbie Duncan
Illustrations by Anita Belli
This edition copyright © 2020 Lion Hudson IP Limited

Published by
Lion Hudson Limited
Wilkinson House, Jordan Hill Business Park
Banbury Road, Oxford OX2 8DR, England
www.lionhudson.com

ISBN 978 1 78128 374 5

First edition 2020

Acknowledgments
Scriptures quotation p. 42 taken from the Good News Bible © 1994 published
by the Bible Societies/HarperCollins Publishers Ltd UK, Good News Bible©
American Bible Society 1966, 1971, 1976, 1992. Used with permission.

A catalogue record for this book is available from the British Library

Printed and bound in China, January 2020, LH54

GOD CARES

WHEN I AM AFRAID

Jesus Calms the Storm

By Debbie Duncan
Illustrated by Anita Belli

CANDLE
BOOKS

About the Series

"In raising healthy children, it's not enough to just focus on the physical aspect of health. To be truly healthy, a child's emotional health must be nurtured and strengthened. Developing a mental attitude of wellness is also essential. When we adopt an attitude of wellness, we take on a belief that being well is a natural, normal state."

Jane Sheppard, "A Wellness Approach for Children", *Aspire* magazine, 9 June 2009

The *God Cares* series is about providing parents with a biblical approach to discussing emotions and behaviour with their children to provide an attitude of wellness. Children of different ages and at different stages of their emotional development approach things differently, so this series works on two separate levels: **readers aimed at five- to seven-year olds, and chapter books aimed at children aged eight and above**. Please note that children progress at different rates in terms of their reading ability and emotional development, so the age ranges are only a guide for parents and carers.

The Bible stories are retold reflecting on the emotions. Children are encouraged to discuss this and relate the stories to their own situations. Sections at the back provide a reflective space for children, and practical advice for parents and carers.

About the Author

Debbie Duncan, the author of *The Art of Daily Resilience* and *Brave*, is a nurse, a teacher, and the mother of four children. Debbie has considerable insight into what constitutes resilience and bravery: the ability to cope, to stay on course, and to bounce back. In her books she considers what is required for physical, mental, and spiritual durability, interweaving biblical teaching and prayers with personal anecdotes and sound advice. This she now applies specifically to support parents and carers raising children.

Introduction

We are going to look at how God cares even when we are afraid. In this story we learn that Jesus' friends became afraid even though Jesus was in the boat with them. They thought they were going to drown.

Sometimes we can be afraid even if our parents or the people we love – and who love us – are with us. Maybe you have gone to the park with them and have been pushed and shoved by lots of people all going where you are going. The people are noisy and you get scared. You forget you are holding your dad's hand. Read the story and then chat with your parents, or those who care for you, about how you feel. There are some questions at the end to help you.

JESUS CALMS THE STORM

Jesus had been so busy
that he was now tired.
He needed to sleep but he was
surrounded by noisy people.
He was famous in the country
where he lived. Wherever he went,
lots of people followed him.

Only a few days before,
a huge crowd of people started
following Jesus. They wanted
to hear what he had to say.
They followed him all the way
to the shore. Jesus and his friends
had to get into a boat and head to
the middle of the sea to escape them.

But the crowds following Jesus
grew bigger and bigger each day.
He was worried he might get hurt.

Jesus was teaching the people about God. Many of them thought that God was only interested in people who always did the right thing.

This is hard to do. We all get things wrong. This made the people sad as they wanted to know God better.

Jesus knew this wasn't true. Jesus told the people God loved them no matter what and they were amazed! They all wanted to hear more.

The people wanted to hear more,

Jesus just wanted to snore,

The people wanted to hear more,

Jesus needed to rest like before.

So, just like before, Jesus decided to get into a boat and head to the other side of the sea to find some peace and quiet. He decided to have a little nap and made himself comfortable. He even had a cushion to lie on.

Jesus' friends were fishermen and knew what they were doing. Jesus left them in charge of the boat. He wasn't worried as he knew God would look after them.

The Sea of Galilee is a huge, deep lake in the middle of a valley. It's so big that people who live near it call it a sea. Sometimes, storms happen quickly and can be really, really scary – especially if you are in a little boat. The waves can be over 3 metres (10 feet) tall!

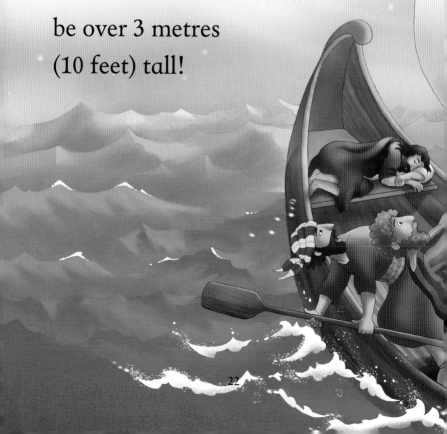

That is nearly as tall as an African elephant or a basketball hoop!

The storm started suddenly, with huge, powerful waves nearly flooding the boat.

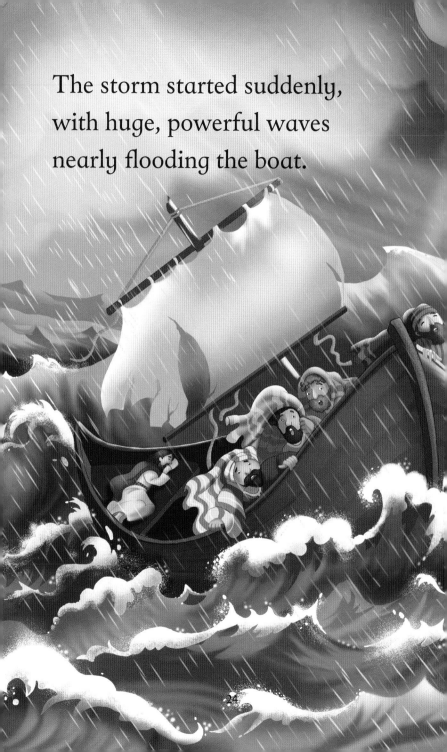

Crashing waves rocked the boat,
Jesus' friends just kept afloat.
They pushed the oars and pulled on ropes,
all were scared and losing hope.

Jesus' friends became afraid, even though Jesus was in the boat with them. They thought they were going to drown.

We don't know exactly what they did, but they would have done everything they could to keep the boat afloat.

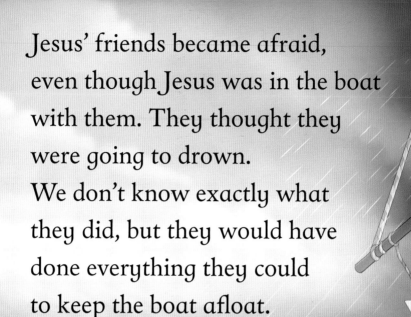

Jesus' friends forgot Jesus was with them in the boat. He was in a deep sleep as he was at peace. He knew God was with him. He knew there was nothing to fear.

The friends were so scared, but then they remembered Jesus was there. They woke Jesus up. "Don't you care if we drown?" they asked him.

What a silly question to ask Jesus!
But the friends were frightened
and that can make us do and say
silly things. Their fear of the storm
made them forget that Jesus did
care. They forgot that God
loved them no matter what.
They forgot they had seen
Jesus do amazing things.

Jesus' friends forgot he loved them,
All they could hear were the waves and the storm,
Jesus' friends forgot he was near,
All they could do was shake with fear.

Jesus heard his friends and stood up.
Jesus told the wind to be still.
He told the sea to be still.
That moment the sea and storm
calmed down.

The sea became as smooth as glass.
The friends were amazed.
They could not believe that the sea
and storm did as Jesus asked!

You may think that story is
amazing. It is amazing!
Jesus wants us to know that he is
with us even when things are scary.
God cares when we are afraid.
Jesus wants us to remember that
he is always holding our hand.

TIME TO TALK

This section is to help you to talk with your parents, or those who care for you, about what you have learned. There are lots of things you can be afraid of. You can fear things that most people don't find scary. When you talk about it, you remember that there are some things we don't need to be afraid of.

What are you afraid of?

It is important to talk to someone you trust about what you are afraid of. They will help you work out what is a real fear and what is an imaginary fear. The disciples even woke Jesus up to tell him what they were afraid of. Maybe like Jesus' friends, the sound of the stormy winds and rain scare you.

Your parents may ask you to talk about your fears and help you remember that Jesus is with you.

When were you last afraid?

Our family has a friend who was really scared of dogs. She was afraid of an animal she had never really met. We had two little dogs called Bilbo and Bessie.When our friend and her family came to our house, we had to lock the dogs away. This went on for quite a long time. Then, one day, she visited and met the dogs. After lots of visits, she soon found she was not afraid of the dogs anymore. She had learned that there was nothing to be afraid of.

Now the family has a dog of its own called Hope!

If you are afraid, then talk to someone you can trust. Even if you think your fear is silly, speak to an adult such as your teacher, your mum or dad, or the person who looks after you.

How did you feel when you were afraid?

Remember the story we have just read. I am sure Jesus didn't want to be woken up, but he still did something to stop his friends being afraid. Remember Jesus is also with you.

YOUR PRAYER SPACE

Loving God,
I am scared of ....
I want to hide here
and not move.

Loving God,
I ask you to be with me today.
I want to put my hand in yours
and move on.

Amen

The Lord is my light
and my salvation;
I will fear no one.
The Lord protects me
from all danger;
I will never be afraid.

(Psalm 27:1)

Advice for Parents and Carers

It's good to remember that fear is a normal human emotion. It's natural for children to feel afraid at times. Fear enables us to be cautious of things we don't understand or have not dealt with before. We also teach our children to be fearful and cautious of specific dangers, such as strangers or crossing the road. In some circumstances fear is a tool that helps us protect children.

There are times, however, when our children are afraid of things that we don't feel are threatening. The reasons for their fears can also change as they get older. They may be afraid of something hiding under the bed or have a fear of the dark. Some of these fears stay with us into adulthood and become irrational fears.

There are some children who are more fearful than others. There are also factors that make some children more sensitive and anxious than other children. Perhaps a family member is an anxious person and this has an impact upon them, or they have been overprotected and not allowed to face everyday fears. Stressful events can also lead to a child becoming very anxious, such as family breakdown or starting a new school.

As your child develops and learns more about the world around them, their list of fears can change. Some fears are real, but some are imaginary. Common fears are of the dark, separation, or monsters. Try to talk about these different fears and put them in context.

Here are some suggestions:

- Let your child know that you are listening to them and take their fears seriously.
- Be honest with your child about the questions they have. If you are also scared of the dark, say so and face it together.
- Let your child confront what they are afraid of. Do it one step at a time. Remember Bilbo and Bessie, and the girl who was afraid of the dogs? As your child starts to face their fear, try to break the association of the strong emotion of fear with the event. For example, if your child is scared of the dark, make shadow shapes to make them laugh.
- Enable your child to feel like they are in control. If they are afraid of monsters under the bed,

get them to check under the bed. (Don't do it with them, however, or they will think it's true.)

- Ask your child what they think would make them feel more secure.
- Ensure your child has a daily timetable – routines and rituals give a child a sense of stability.
- Remain consistent in your approach to your child's fear.
- Limit your child's exposure to things that can scare them such as certain movies or books.
- Let your child know you believe in them.
- Pray with your child about their fears.

If you feel that your child's fears and anxieties are getting worse, talk to someone who can help you. Your general practitioner or school can offer advice. They will know someone who can help. Also speak to your child's church worker. In some cases you may need to find out why your child has developed the fear they have. You may need to get further help to do that. And always end these conversations praying to the one who calms the storm and reminds us he is with us all the time. God cares.

Resources

Association of Christian Counsellors:
https://www.acc-uk.org/find-a-counsellor/
search-for-a-counsellor.html

Care for the Family – parent support:
https://www.careforthefamily.org.uk/family-
life/parent-support

National Health Service:
https://www.nhs.uk/conditions/stress-anxiety-
depression/anxiety-in-children/

Other Titles in the Series

Readers

God Cares When I am Strong: Friends in the Fire

Chapter Books

*God Cares When I Feel Down: Jonah and Other
Stories*

*God Cares When I am Anxious: Moses and Other
Stories*

Acknowledgments

I want to thank my husband Malcolm, Matthew and Eve, Benjamin and Ellie, Anna and Jacob, Riodhna, Rob and Emily – our family – for all their love and care while writing this series.

I also want to thank Anita Belli who is so gifted at illustration and captured what I was trying to say.

I also want to thank the Lion Hudson family: Suzanne Wilson-Higgins for that initial conversation, commissioning editor Deborah Lock for her patience, Jacqui Crawford for the design and layout, and Stella Caldwell and Eva Rojas for advice and poetry help on the readers (some of the lines are Eva's). You are just a few of the family!

Thank you.